T0119789

WHISKEY
COCKTAILS

WHISKEY COCKTAILS

40 recipes for Old Fashioneds, Sours,
Manhattans, Juleps and more

Jesse Estes

photography by Alex Luck

RYLAND PETERS & SMALL
LONDON • NEW YORK

To my family, for always being a source of inspiration and support.

Designers Sonya Nathoo and Toni Kay
Commissioning Editor Alice Sambrook
Production Manager Mai-Ling Collyer
Editorial Director Julia Charles
Art Director Leslie Harrington
Publisher Cindy Richards

Drinks Stylist Tara Garnell
Prop Stylist Luis Peral
Indexer Vanessa Bird

First published in 2018 as *From Dram to Manhattan*. This revised edition published in 2021 by
Ryland Peters & Small
20–21 Jockey's Fields
London WC1R 4BW
and
341 E 116th Street
New York, 10029

www.rylandpeters.com

10 9 8 7 6 5 4 3

ISBN: 978-1-78879-387-2

A CIP record for this book is available from the British Library. US Library of Congress CIP data has been applied for.

Printed in China

Notes:
- Each cocktail recipe serves 1 unless otherwise stated.
- Edible flowers must be food-safe and pesticide-free.
- Raw egg whites should not be fed to the very young, pregnant, elderly or anyone with a compromised immune system.

A note on spelling: In general, Scotch, Canadian and Japanese are spelled 'whisky,' while American and Irish are spelled 'whiskey' (there are exceptions to this rule; for instance, Maker's Mark – a bourbon – spells 'whisky' without the 'e' on its label). (Whisk(e)y is produced in dozens more countries but the aforementioned are the most well-known types globally.)

CONTENTS

Introduction 6

Old Fashioneds 9

Sours & Short Drinks 17

Manhattans 27

Juleps 39

Highballs & Long Drinks 47

Happy Endings 57

Index & Credits 64

INTRODUCTION

'Too much of anything is bad, but too much good whiskey is barely enough.'

Mark Twain

The word 'whisky' comes from the Gaelic word usquebaugh (uisge beatha in Scottish Gaelic), meaning 'water of life'. Whisk(e)y shares its etymology with many other spirits: aqua vitae (Latin), eau de vie (French), akvavit (Scandinavian) – all translating to 'water of life'. Like many spirits, they are referring to the pursuit of the 'elixir of life'.

Today, many popular classic whisk(e)y cocktails tend to be bourbon-based (such as the old fashioned, manhattan, mint julep, whiskey sour, etc), but there are some great Scotch and Irish whisk(e)y drinks too (blue blazer, morning glory fizz, etc). Japanese whisky, a fairly new category, still has relatively few cocktails and purists will often assert that it should be consumed neat, mizuwari (with water) or as a highball. I've included some new Japanese whisky cocktails in this book, since the spirit does lend itself perfectly to mixing as well as sipping neat. For those who are new to the world of whisk(e)y, I have compiled a short breakdown of the varieties available, so that you can understand the spirits you are mixing and partake in the connoisseur culture surrounding this cult spirit.

AMERICAN WHISKEYS

These are normally made from up to four different grains: corn, rye, wheat and barley. The selection of these grains used is referred to as the 'mash bill'. The following three categories must all be aged in brand-new, charred, American white oak barrels for at least 2 years (although most will have spent at least 4 years). American whiskeys are generally characterized by their sweet and spicy flavour profiles, which can include hints of coconut, toffee and vanilla. Bourbon is the best-known type of American whiskey, but there is much more to this category besides.

Bourbon

This must have a minimum of 51% corn content in the mash bill. Bourbon is generally characterized by its particularly sweet vanilla and caramel notes. A common misconception is that bourbon's production is limited to Kentucky; it can in fact legally be made anywhere in the United States.

Straight Rye Whiskey

Straight rye needs to have a minimum content of 51% rye in the mash bill. Currently a very trendy category, American rye whiskey offers a nuttier, spicier and drier flavour profile than bourbon.

Tennessee Straight Whiskey

The best-selling brand of American whiskey, Jack Daniel's, employs a type of filtration process known as the Lincoln County Process, during which the unaged whiskey is filtered through 3 meters/10 ft of maple charcoal before being barrelled. Bourbon is not legally allowed to be filtered before aging, which means that Jack Daniel's cannot call themselves 'bourbon'.

NEW MAKE/'WHITE DOG'

This is unaged American whiskey that uses either a predominantly corn or rye mash bill. White Dog is increasingly trendy these days with bartenders and consumers alike.

SCOTCH WHISKY

Scotch must be aged for a minimum of 3 years and is commonly aged in former American whiskey barrels, but sherry and other types of used casks will also often be utilized. In general, Scotch is double-distilled. There are five different classifications for Scotch: Single Malt, Single Grain, Blended Malt, Blended Grain and Blended Scotch. There are five official Scotch regions: Highlands & Islands, Islay (famous for its smoky, peaty and salty whiskies), Lowlands, Speyside (the largest Scotch-producing region) and Campbeltown.

IRISH WHISKEY

This also needs to be aged for a minimum of 3 years, but in contrast to Scotch, it is generally distilled three times. While 'blended' whiskey is the most common type of Irish whiskey, there is also 'single pot still' whiskey – meaning that it was made at a single distillery from a pot still, using both malted and unmalted barley. Until fairly recently, there were only three distilleries producing Irish whiskey. Newcomers to the category include brands like Teeling.

JAPANESE WHISKY

The newest category of whisky included in this book, Japanese whisky is increasingly sought-after. It was first produced in the early 1920s at Suntory's Yamazaki Distillery. Masataka Taketsuru is credited as being the creator of Japanese whisky – he studied whisky production in Scotland and returned to begin producing in Japan. While Japanese whisky production was originally modelled on Scotch, their methods have since evolved, and the result is a very wide variety of flavour profiles, often very different from Scotch.

OLD FASHIONEDS

Old Fashioned

One of the most popular cocktails of all time, this drink is likely the 'original cocktail' - in the sense that the oldest recorded recipe we have for a cocktail lists the ingredients as a base spirit, bitters, sugar and water (or ice). The old fashioned has come back in vogue in recent years, thanks to vintage-style popular culture influences such as the *Mad Men* TV series.

**7.5 ml/1$^{1}/_{2}$ teaspoons simple Demerara/
turbinado sugar syrup**

3 dashes Angostura bitters

60 ml/2 fl oz Michter's Bourbon

large strip of orange zest, to garnish

Combine all the drink ingredients in a mixing glass with a large scoop of cubed ice and stir for 20–30 seconds. Strain into a rocks glass over cubed ice. Squeeze the orange zest over the top of the drink to express the citrus oils, then drop into the glass to garnish.

Benton's Old Fashioned

Created by Don Lee in 2008 at the world-famous PDT bar in New York City, this drink quickly became popular in cocktail bars across the globe. The combination of bourbon, bacon and maple syrup works perfectly. (Not suitable for vegetarians!)

7.5 ml/1^{1}/$_{2}$ teaspoons grade B maple syrup

60 ml/2 fl oz Bacon Fat-washed Four Roses Yellow Label Bourbon*

2 dashes Angostura bitters

large strip of orange zest, to garnish

Combine all the drink ingredients in a mixing glass and stir until the maple syrup is amalgamated with the bourbon and Angostura bitters. Add a scoop of cubed ice and stir for about 20 seconds before straining into a rocks glass over cubed ice. Garnish with a large strip of orange zest dropped into the glass.

* To make Bacon Fat-washed Bourbon: 45 ml/1^{1}/$_{2}$ fl oz bacon fat, 750 ml/3^{1}/$_{4}$ cups Four Roses Yellow Label Bourbon

Heat the bacon fat in a saucepan over a low heat until melted. Stir together the melted fat and bourbon in a jug/pitcher and let infuse at room temperature for 4 hours. Cover and freeze for 2 hours. Remove the fat solids by straining the liquid through a fine-mesh sieve/strainer or muslin/cheesecloth and discard. Store the bacon fat-washed bourbon in a sealed bottle at room temperature and use within 1 month.

Sazerac

The sazerac hails back to the mid-1800s and is said to have been created at the Sazerac Coffee House in New Orleans. The original sazerac cocktail was probably made with brandy, but has since evolved to more commonly use rye whiskey, as I have done here. You can also experiment with trying equal parts rye and brandy (30 ml/1 fl oz each) as the base.

5 ml/1 teaspoon absinthe, for the glass 'rinse'
60 ml/2 fl oz Sazerac Rye Whiskey
5 ml/1 teaspoon simple Demerara/turbinado sugar syrup
3 dashes Peychaud's bitters
large strip of lemon zest, to serve

Add the absinthe to a small rocks glass filled with crushed ice and leave the glass to chill while preparing the drink. Combine the rye whiskey, Demerara/turbinado sugar syrup and bitters in a mixing glass with a scoop of cubed ice and stir for about 30 seconds. Discard the crushed ice and absinthe from the rocks glass before straining the drink into the chilled, absinthe-rinsed rocks glass. Squeeze the lemon zest to express the citrus oils over the top and sides of the glass, before discarding the zest.

The Kingpin

Japan meets Kentucky in this salted caramel old fashioned.

60 ml/2 fl oz Nikka Whisky
From The Barrel

5 ml/1 teaspoon Salted Caramel
Syrup*

10 ml/2 teaspoons coconut water

2 dashes Fee Brothers Whiskey
Barrel-Aged Bitters

lemon and orange zests, to garnish

Combine all the drink ingredients in a double old fashioned glass with a scoop
of cubed ice. Stir for about 45 seconds or until diluted to your desire. Squeeze
the citrus zests over the glass to express the oils and use to garnish the drink.

* To make Salted Caramel Syrup: 500 g/2$^{1}/_{2}$ cups caster/granulated sugar,
500 ml/2 cups hot water, 1 heaped tablespoon sea salt

Combine the sugar, half the hot water and the salt in a saucepan and bring to
the boil. Stir until the sugar has dissolved. Reduce the heat and simmer without
stirring for 10–20 minutes until amber in colour. Carefully add the remaining
250 ml/1 cup of hot water and stir to combine. Let cool before bottling.
Keep the syrup refrigerated and use within 1 month.

Prohibition Old Fashioned

This is the preferred iteration of 'King Cocktail' Dale DeGroff.

5 ml/1 teaspoon simple sugar syrup

1 Luxardo maraschino cherry, plus
5 ml/1 teaspoon syrup (from cherry jar)

3 dashes Angostura bitters

1 orange wheel

60 ml/2 fl oz Jefferson's Reserve
Bourbon

1 splash soda water

orange zest and a fresh cherry,
to garnish

Combine all the drink ingredients, except the bourbon and soda water, in the
base of a cocktail shaker and muddle. Add the bourbon and some cubed ice and
shake hard for less than 6 seconds. Fine-strain into an old fashioned glass over
cubed ice. Add the soda water and garnish with orange zest and a cherry.

SOURS & SHORT DRINKS

Whiskey Sour

Along with the old fashioned and manhattan, the whiskey sour is another quintessential American whiskey cocktail, which has evolved to include a whole family of derivative drinks. The combination of bourbon, lemon, sugar, bitters and egg white is unbeatable, and the reason this drink remains so popular in bars around the world today.

50 ml/1²/₃ fl oz Woodford Reserve Bourbon

25 ml/³/₄ fl oz fresh lemon juice

25 ml/³/₄ fl oz simple sugar syrup

20 ml/²/₃ fl oz egg white

3 dashes Angostura bitters, plus extra to garnish

lemon slice and Luxardo maraschino cherry, to garnish

Combine all the drink ingredients in a cocktail shaker and 'dry' shake first with no ice to emulsify the egg white. Add a scoop of cubed ice and shake vigorously. Strain into a rocks glass over cubed ice and garnish with a lemon slice, Luxardo maraschino cherry and an extra dash of Angostura bitters.

New York Sour

A red wine float provides a delectable twist on the classic whiskey sour.

50 ml/1^2/$_3$ fl oz Bulleit Bourbon

25 ml/^{3}/$_4$ fl oz fresh lemon juice

25 ml/^{3}/$_4$ fl oz simple sugar syrup

1 dash Angostura bitters

20 ml/^{2}/$_3$ fl oz egg white

25 ml/^{3}/$_4$ fl oz red wine

edible flower, to garnish

Combine all the drink ingredients, except the wine, in a cocktail shaker and 'dry' shake without ice to emulsify the egg white. Add a scoop of cubed ice, then shake hard and strain into a small wine glass over cubed ice. Pour the red wine slowly over the back of a bar spoon or teaspoon to 'float' a layer of red wine over the cocktail. Garnish with an edible flower.

Ward Eight

Named after a voting district in Boston famous for its political corruption, the ward eight is a somewhat forgotten classic cocktail that shows how well rye whiskey can pair with orange juice.

50 ml/1^2/$_3$ fl oz Michter's Straight Rye Whiskey

25 ml/^{3}/$_4$ fl oz fresh lemon juice

25 ml/^{3}/$_4$ fl oz fresh orange juice

7.5 ml/1^1/$_2$ teaspoons grenadine

10 ml/2 teaspoons simple sugar syrup (or to taste)

orange wedge and Luxardo maraschino cherry, to garnish

Add all the drink ingredients to a cocktail shaker with a scoop of cubed ice and shake hard. Strain into a chilled coupe glass and garnish with an orange wedge and a cherry.

Paper Plane

Created by bartender Sam Ross, this cocktail fast became a modern classic. The sum is even greater than this drink's four equal parts.

25 ml/³/4 fl oz Woodford Reserve Bourbon

25 ml/³/4 fl oz fresh lemon juice

25 ml/³/4 fl oz Aperol

25 ml/³/4 fl oz Amaro Nonino

Combine all the drink ingredients in a cocktail shaker with a scoop of cubed iced and shake hard. Double-strain into a coupe glass and garnish with an origami paper plane on a cocktail stick or mini peg.

Blood and Sand

While the original recipe was equal parts of the four ingredients, this recipe seems to be better adapted to modern palates. Using fresh orange juice is key, but you may need to adjust the ratios slightly depending on the sweetness or acidity of the orange.

30 ml/1 fl oz Chivas Regal 12 Year Old Blended Scotch

20 ml/²/3 fl oz Punt e Mes, or other sweet vermouth

25 ml/³/4 fl oz Heering Cherry Liqueur

25 ml/³/4 fl oz fresh orange juice

flaming orange zest coin (optional), to garnish

Add all the drink ingredients to a cocktail shaker with a scoop of cubed ice and shake hard. Double-strain into a coupe glass. If you want to make a flaming orange zest garnish, light a match and hold it about 8 cm/3 inches above the surface of the drink. Carefully hold the orange zest coin over the flame, angled down towards the drink to heat for a few seconds. Squeeze the zest to release the citrus oils and ignite them, creating a flare over the drink. Drop the zest face up into the drink. Alternatively, simply garnish the glass with the orange zest.

Penicillin

Another drink created by Sam Ross, it's no surprise this cocktail was an instant winner when he came up with the recipe in 2005 at New York City bar Milk & Honey. The smokiness of the Scotch combines perfectly with lemon, honey and ginger. This drink works equally well as a winter warmer to soothe sore throats or as a summer cooler to beat the heat.

50 ml/1^2/$_3$ fl oz Chivas Regal 12 Year Old Blended Scotch

25 ml/^{3}/$_4$ fl oz fresh lemon juice

25 ml/^{3}/$_4$ fl oz Honey Ginger Syrup*

10 ml/2 teaspoons Laphroaig 10 Year Old Single Malt Scotch

candied ginger and lemon wedge, to garnish

Combine all the drink ingredients in a cocktail shaker with a scoop of cubed ice and shake hard. Strain into a rocks glass over cubed ice. Garnish with candied ginger and a lemon wedge.

* To make Honey Ginger Syrup: 250 ml/^{3}/$_4$ cup runny honey, 15-cm/6-inch piece of fresh ginger, peeled and sliced, 250 ml/1 cup water

Stir together all the ingredients in a saucepan and bring to the boil. Reduce to a simmer for 5 minutes. Let the syrup cool then remove the solids using a fine-mesh sieve/strainer or muslin/cheesecloth and discard. Store the syrup in a sealed bottle in the fridge and use within 1 month.

Lion's Tail

This largely forgotten classic cocktail was first published in the Café Royal Cocktail Book in 1937. I've simply added some Yellow Chartreuse to the basic recipe as the herbaceous and saffron notes interplay beautifully with the bourbon and pimento dram.

45 ml/1½ fl oz Wild Turkey 80 Proof Bourbon

25 ml/¾ fl oz fresh lime juice

17.5 ml/3½ teaspoons simple sugar syrup

10 ml/2 teaspoons Yellow Chartreuse

5 dashes pimento dram (allspice liqueur)

lime zest, to garnish

Combine all the drink ingredients in a cocktail shaker with a scoop of cubed ice and shake hard. Strain into a chilled coupe glass and garnish with lime zest.

Honi Honi

Honi honi means 'kiss kiss' in Tahitian. This is essentially a mai tai with bourbon instead of rum. It's superbly refreshing and dangerously easy to drink!

50 ml/1⅔ fl oz Buffalo Trace Bourbon

25 ml/¾ fl oz fresh lime juice

15 ml/½ fl oz Cointreau

15 ml/½ fl oz orgeat (almond syrup)

fresh pineapple spear, fresh mint sprig, orange slice, Luxardo maraschino cherry and icing/confectioners' sugar, to garnish

Combine all the drink ingredients in a cocktail shaker with a scoop of cubed ice and shake. Strain into a tiki mug or rocks glass over crushed ice. Cap the glass with more crushed ice and garnish with a pineapple spear, mint sprig, orange slice and cherry. Dust with icing/confectioners' sugar to finish.

MANHATTANS

Sweet Manhattan

Perhaps one of the most iconic cocktails of all time, there is a reason that the manhattan is a tried-and-true classic. Bourbon pairs beautifully with sweet vermouth and bitters: together they are a match made in heaven. The manhattan is also the basis for countless variations - for instance substitute bourbon for Scotch and you've got a rob roy.

50 ml/²/₃ fl oz Jefferson's Reserve Bourbon

25 ml/³/₄ fl oz Cocchi Vermouth di Torino, or other sweet vermouth

3 dashes Angostura bitters

orange zest, to serve

Luxardo maraschino cherry, to garnish

Combine all the drink ingredients in a mixing glass with a scoop of cubed ice. Stir for about 30 seconds before straining into a chilled coupette glass. Squeeze the orange zest to express the citrus oils over the drink and discard. Garnish with a Luxardo maraschino cherry.

Black Manhattan

This twist on the manhattan foregoes vermouth, putting Amaro Averna front and centre. The recipe is adapted from a cocktail created by Todd Smith at Bourbon & Branch in San Francisco.

60 ml/2 fl oz Bulleit Rye Whiskey

15 ml/^{1}/$_2$ fl oz Amaro Averna

15 ml/^{1}/$_2$ fl oz amontillado sherry

5 ml/1 teaspoon Pedro Ximénez sherry

2 dashes Bittermens Xocolatl (chocolate) Mole Bitters

orange zest and a fresh pitted cherry, to garnish

Combine all the drink ingredients in a mixing glass with a scoop of cubed ice. Stir for about 20 seconds before straining into a chilled coupe glass. Squeeze the orange zest to express the citrus oils over the drink. Garnish the glass with the orange zest and a fresh pitted cherry dropped into the drink.

Brooklyn

A variation of the manhattan named after the neighbouring borough. Replace the Amer Picon with Cynar, and you've got a bensonhurst, an equally delectable cocktail.

45 ml/1^1/$_2$ fl oz Rittenhouse 100 Proof Rye Whiskey

15 ml/^{1}/$_2$ fl oz Noilly Prat Dry, or other dry vermouth

5 ml/1 teaspoon Amer Picon

5 ml/1 teaspoon Luxardo Maraschino Cherry Liqueur

lemon zest, to serve

Luxardo maraschino cherry, to garnish

Combine all the drink ingredients in a mixing glass with a scoop of cubed ice. Stir for about 30 seconds before straining into a chilled coupette glass. Squeeze the lemon zest to express the citrus oils over the drink and discard. Garnish with a cherry.

Remember the Maine

High-proof rye whiskey, vermouth, cherry and aniseed from the absinthe combine here wonderfully to create a moreish sipper.

50 ml/1²/₃ fl oz Rittenhouse
100 Proof Rye Whiskey

20 ml/²/₃ fl oz Punt e Mes, or other
sweet vermouth

7.5 ml/1¹/₂ teaspoons Heering
Cherry Liqueur

3 dashes absinthe

lemon zest, to serve

Luxardo maraschino cherry,
to garnish

Combine all the drink ingredients in a mixing glass with a scoop of cubed ice. Stir for around 30 seconds before straining into a chilled martini glass. Squeeze the lemon zest to express the citrus oils over the top and sides of the glass. Discard the lemon zest and garnish with a Luxardo maraschino cherry.

Boulevardier

The original recipe for the boulevardier was equal parts bourbon, Campari and sweet vermouth (essentially a bourbon Negroni), but I prefer a 3:1:1 ratio, effectively making a manhattan-style cocktail. To make an old pal cocktail, replace the sweet vermouth with dry vermouth, and the bourbon with rye whiskey.

45 ml/1¹/₂ fl oz Four Roses Small
Batch Bourbon

15 ml/¹/₂ fl oz Carpano Antica
Formula, or other sweet vermouth

15 ml/¹/₂ fl oz Campari

orange zest coin, to garnish

Stir all the drink ingredients together in a mixing glass with a scoop of cubed ice for around 30 seconds. Strain into a chilled coupette glass and garnish with an orange zest coin.

White Manhattan

Unaged American whiskey (nicknamed 'white dog') has gained cult status in recent years. This drink uses Georgia Moon whiskey and other 'white' ingredients for a variation on the manhattan.

40 ml/1^1/$_3$ fl oz Georgia Moon Corn Whiskey

20 ml/^{2}/$_3$ fl oz Cocchi Americano (aromatized wine)

3 dashes white wine vinegar

10 ml/2 teaspoons Suze (bitters flavoured with gentian root)

1 dash Regan's Orange Bitters

lemon zest, to garnish

Stir all the drink ingredients together in a mixing glass with a scoop of cubed ice for around 20–30 seconds. Strain into a chilled coupe glass. Squeeze the lemon zest to express the citrus oils over the top and sides of the drink and use to garnish the glass.

Vieux Carré

Pronounced 'voo ka-ray', the name of this drink translates to 'old square', the French term for New Orleans' French Quarter.

30 ml/1 fl oz Sazerac Rye Whiskey

30 ml/1 fl oz Cognac

30 ml/1 fl oz Martini Rosso, or other sweet vermouth

7.5 ml/1^1/$_2$ teaspoons Benedictine

1 dash Angostura bitters

1 dash Peychaud's bitters

large strip of lemon zest, to garnish

Stir all the drink ingredients together in a mixing glass with a scoop of cubed ice for around 15–20 seconds. Strain into a rocks glass over cubed ice. Squeeze the lemon zest to express the citrus oils over the top and sides of the drink and use to garnish the glass.

Bobby Burns

This twist on the rob roy was named after Scottish poet Robert Burns. To add extra depth to the drink, try including a dash of absinthe and/or orange bitters. The smokiness of the Scotch works perfectly with the herbaceous and spicy notes of the Benedictine.

50 ml/1^2/$_3$ fl oz Glenmorangie The Original Single Malt Scotch Whisky

25 ml/^{3}/$_4$ fl oz Martini Rosso, or other sweet vermouth

12.5 ml/2^1/$_2$ teaspoons Benedictine

lemon zest, to garnish

Combine all the drink ingredients in a mixing glass with a scoop of cubed ice. Stir for about 30 seconds before straining into a chilled coupette glass. Squeeze the lemon zest to express the citrus oils over the drink before using to garnish the glass.

Tipperary

This drink first appeared in print in a cocktail book written by Hugo R. Ensslin in 1916. His original recipe called for equal parts Irish whiskey, Chartreuse and sweet vermouth. A slightly altered version appeared in Harry MacElhone's *Harry's ABC of Mixing Cocktails*, published in 1922. With less Chartreuse and vermouth, the whiskey is given more prominence, creating a taste better suited to today's palates. The herbaceous notes from the Chartreuse complement the Irish Teeling Whiskey perfectly.

50 ml/1²/₃ fl oz Teeling Whiskey
25 ml/³/₄ fl oz Carpano Antica Formula, or other sweet vermouth
10 ml/2 teaspoons Green Chartreuse
2 dashes Angostura bitters
orange zest, to garnish

Combine all the drink ingredients in a mixing glass with a scoop of cubed ice. Stir for about 30 seconds before straining into a chilled coupette glass. Squeeze the orange zest to express the citrus oils over the drink before adding as a garnish to the glass.

JULEPS

Mint Julep

This Kentucky Derby mainstay originated in the American South in the 18th century. There are very few things as refreshing as the numbingly cold mixture of mint, sugar and bourbon churned with crushed ice on a hot summer's day. Beware though, because it is all too easy to drink and deceptively strong!

8–10 fresh mint leaves

25 ml/^{3}/$_4$ fl oz simple sugar syrup

75 ml/2^1/$_2$ fl oz Michter's Bourbon

3–4 fresh mint sprigs, to garnish

Combine the mint leaves and syrup in a julep tin or tumbler and muddle gently to release the oils (muddling the mint leaves too heavily will release bitter chlorophyll, so be gentle!). Add the bourbon, then fill the tin up with crushed ice. Stir all the ingredients together for about 30 seconds, until the outside of the tin is frosted. Cap the top of the drink with more crushed ice and garnish with mint sprigs. Serve with a straw.

Derby Julep

This refreshing quaff is a cross between a brown derby (bourbon, grapefruit and honey) and a classic mint julep.

7.5 ml/1^1/$_2$ teaspoons runny honey (or to taste)

8 fresh mint leaves

60 ml/2 fl oz Eagle Rare Bourbon

30 ml/1 fl oz fresh pink grapefruit juice

5 ml/1 teaspoon orgeat (almond syrup)

fresh mint sprig and pink grapefruit slices cut into a fan, to garnish

Combine the honey and mint leaves in the base of a highball glass. Muddle the mint very gently to release its oils. Add all the other ingredients and fill the glass with crushed ice. Stir together for about 20–30 seconds. Garnish the drink with a large mint sprig and fresh pink grapefruit slice 'fan'. Serve with a straw.

Georgia Mint Julep

Bourbon, mint and peach is another winning combination (even though the original recipe calls for brandy). For another variation, try substituting peach liqueur for apricot brandy.

8 fresh mint leaves

2 dashes Fee Brothers Whiskey Barrel-Aged Bitters (or Angostura)

25 ml/^{3}/$_4$ fl oz Merlet Crème de Pêche

75 ml/2^1/$_2$ fl oz W.L. Weller 12 Year Old Bourbon

2–3 large fresh mint sprigs, 2 fresh or frozen peach slices and icing/confectioners' sugar, to garnish

Combine the mint leaves, bitters and crème de pêche in a julep tin or tumbler and muddle gently to release the oils. Add the bourbon, then fill the tin with crushed ice. Stir all the ingredients together for about 30 seconds, until the outside of the tin is frosted. Cap the top of the drink with crushed ice and garnish with mint sprigs and peach slices. Dust with icing/confectioners' sugar to finish and serve with a straw.

Triple Crown Julep

Pecans and bourbon are a great match. This julep is a nice option to enjoy in the winter by a cosy fireplace.

12 fresh mint leaves

12.5 ml/2^{1}/$_{2}$ teaspoons Dark Muscovado Sugar Syrup*

75 ml/2^{1}/$_{2}$ fl oz Pecan Fat-washed W.L. Weller Bourbon**

15 ml/^{1}/$_{2}$ fl oz amontillado sherry

1 dash Fee Brothers Black Walnut Bitters

fresh mint sprigs and candied pecans, to garnish

Combine the mint and muscovado sugar syrup in a julep tin or tumbler and muddle gently to release the oils. Add the bourbon, sherry and bitters, then fill the tin up with crushed ice. Churn until the ingredients are chilled and the drink is slightly diluted, around 30 seconds. Cap with more crushed ice and garnish with mint and candied pecans.

*To make Dark Muscovado Sugar Syrup: 500 ml/2 cups boiling water, 500 g/ 2^{1}/$_{2}$ cups dark muscovado sugar

Combine the boiling water and sugar in a jug/pitcher. Stir until the sugar has dissolved. Let cool before bottling and refrigerating. Use within 1 month.

**To make Pecan Fat-washed Bourbon: 100 g/1 stick salted butter, 150 g/ 1^{1}/$_{2}$ cups lightly crushed pecans, 1 heaped tablespoon Demerara/turbinado sugar, 1 bottle (700–750 ml/3–3^{1}/$_{4}$ cups) W.L. Weller 12 Year Old Bourbon

Heat the butter in a small saucepan over a medium heat until it starts to bubble and brown. Add the pecans and sugar, then stir continuously over a low heat for 2–3 minutes. Remove from the heat and transfer the mixture to a jug/ pitcher or large mason jar containing the bottle of bourbon. Leave to infuse for 1 hour before placing in the freezer overnight. The next day, strain to remove the solids and discard. Bottle and store the pecan fat-washed bourbon at room temperature for up to 1 month.

(**Tip:** save the bourbon-pecan butter and use on pancakes. The bourbon-infused butter pecans are also delicious as a snack or used in a dessert.)

Whiskey Smash

Not technically part of the julep family, but because it includes mint, bourbon and sugar it is not a large deviation. The best part about the whiskey smash is its versatility - try playing around with different fruits that are in season. The original recipe does not include berries, but I find this drink works well with fresh fruit.

1 lemon, cut into eighths

2 fresh blackberries

8 fresh mint leaves

75 ml/2$\frac{1}{2}$ fl oz Old Forester Bourbon

25 ml/$\frac{3}{4}$ fl oz simple sugar syrup

fresh mint sprig, lemon slice and a fresh blackberry, to garnish

Muddle the lemon, blackberries and mint leaves gently in the base of a jam/mason jar, making sure to extract the juice from the lemon wedges. Add the bourbon and syrup and fill the jar with cracked (or a mix of half cubed and half crushed) ice. Close the lid tightly and shake the jar vigorously for 10–12 seconds. Open the lid and cap the glass with crushed ice. Garnish with a mint sprig, lemon slice and a blackberry.

Serve with a straw.

HIGHBALLS
& LONG DRINKS

Whisky Highball

Japanese whisky is a relative newcomer to the scene, but has been making a big splash of late, becoming trendy in bars around Europe and North America and commanding high price tags for bottlings. The highball is believed by many to be the best way to enjoy Japanese whisky (along with drinking it neat or with water). Although on paper it looks simple, making the perfect highball in Japan is akin to an art form, with each bar having its own subtly different technique.

60 ml/2 fl oz Nikka Taketsuru Pure Malt Whisky

soda water, to top up

lemon and/or orange zest or fresh mint sprig (optional), to garnish

Fill a highball glass with large, clear ice cubes and carefully pour the whisky down the side of the glass so that it does not touch the top of the ice. Add the soda slowly in the same manner and stop filling once the soda reaches around 1 cm/^{1}/$_3$ inch from the top of the glass. Use a bar spoon to mix the whisky and soda by placing the spoon between the ice and glass and moving the spoon up and down or in a circular motion for about 5–10 seconds. Serve without a straw. Garnish with citrus zest or a mint sprig to add aroma to the drink.

Bourbon Spritz

Bright and fresh, this drink is the perfect pre-prandial tipple.

20 ml/^{2}/$_3$ fl oz Maker's 46 Bourbon

20 ml/^{2}/$_3$ fl oz fresh pink
grapefruit juice

2 lemon wedges

10 ml/2 teaspoons Goji Berry Syrup*

5 ml/1 teaspoon Campari

75 ml/2^1/$_2$ fl oz Prosecco

50 ml/1^2/$_3$ fl oz soda water

fresh rosemary sprig and grapefruit
zest, to garnish

Combine all the drink ingredients in a large wine glass over cubed ice and stir gently for 5–10 seconds to combine. Garnish with a rosemary sprig and grapefruit zest.

* To make Goji Berry Syrup: 500 ml/2 cups water, 250 g/2^1/$_4$ cups dried goji berries, 500 g/2^1/$_2$ cups caster/granulated sugar

Bring the water to the boil in a saucepan and add the goji berries. Remove from the heat and allow to infuse for a few minutes. Strain out the berries and discard. Stir in the sugar until dissolved. Let cool before bottling and refrigerating. Use within 1 month.

Marquee

Proof that bourbon can do long and fruity drinks too, this recipe was adapted from a cocktail created by Giovanni Burdi at Match Bar, London in 1998.

45 ml/1^1/$_2$ fl oz Maker's Mark Bourbon

45 ml/1^1/$_2$ fl oz cranberry juice

15 ml/^{1}/$_2$ fl oz Chambord Black
Raspberry Liqueur

15 ml/^{1}/$_2$ fl oz fresh lemon juice

10 ml/2 teaspoons simple sugar syrup

3 fresh raspberries

10 ml/2 teaspoons egg white

lemon zest and a fresh raspberry, to garnish

Combine all the drink ingredients in a cocktail shaker and 'dry' shake first with no ice to emulsify the egg white. Add some cubed ice and shake hard. Strain into a highball glass over cubed ice and garnish with lemon zest and a raspberry.

Morning Glory Fizz

This drink originated in the late 1800s and was likely designed
as a hangover cure. The silky smooth texture will soothe your
'morning after' headache and provide an easy-to-drink
hair of the dog that bit you.

60 ml/2 fl oz Chivas Regal 12 Year Old Blended Scotch

12.5 ml/2$^{1}/_{2}$ teaspoons fresh lemon juice

12.5 ml/2$^{1}/_{2}$ teaspoons fresh lime juice

25 ml/$^{3}/_{4}$ fl oz simple sugar syrup

1 dash absinthe

15 ml/$^{1}/_{2}$ fl oz egg white

soda water, to top up

Combine all the ingredients, except the soda water, in a cocktail shaker with a
scoop of cubed ice and shake very hard for at least 30 seconds. Strain into a fizz
glass (or small highball) without ice and top up with soda water, creating
a foamy head on the top of the drink. Serve with no garnish.

Horse's Neck with a Kick

Dating back to the late 19th century, this drink was originally non-alcoholic and simply called a 'horse's neck'. Eventually, someone decided the drink was improved by adding bourbon and it became known as horse's neck 'with a kick'. It's simple, easy to make and very refreshing.

60 ml/2 fl oz Wild Turkey 101 Bourbon

3 dashes Angostura bitters

Fever Tree Ginger Ale, to top up

lemon zest, to garnish

Combine all the drink ingredients in a highball glass over cubed ice. Stir for 5–10 seconds to combine the ingredients, chill and dilute the drink. Garnish with a long spiral of lemon zest.

Whisky Green Tea

This is a very popular drink in China, usually made using Scotch as a base. I find Japanese whisky works equally well.

45 ml/1^1/$_2$ fl oz Mars Maltage "Cosmo" Whisky

120 ml/4 fl oz cold Green Tea*

5 ml/1 teaspoon simple sugar syrup (or to taste)

orange and lemon zests, to garnish

Combine all the drink ingredients in a highball glass over cubed ice. Stir to mix and chill the drink for 10–15 seconds and enjoy cold. Garnish with orange and lemon zests.

*To make Green Tea: 4 green tea bags or loose green tea, 1 litre/quart boiling water

Steep the green tea in the boiling water for around 5 minutes. Remove the tea bags (if using) and let cool before bottling and refrigerating. Use within 3 days.

Whisky Colada

Who says the piña colada should be reserved for rum drinkers? The Chartreuse provides herbal accents in this fruity cocktail.

45 ml/1^1/$_2$ fl oz Nikka Coffey Malt Whisky

20 ml/^{2}/$_3$ fl oz fresh lemon juice

20 ml/^{2}/$_3$ fl oz pineapple juice

20 ml/^{2}/$_3$ fl oz Coco Lopez, or other coconut cream

15 ml/^{1}/$_2$ fl oz Calvados

5 ml/1 teaspoon Green Chartreuse

1 dash Angostura bitters

dehydrated apple slice, desiccated/dried coconut, pineapple spear and a fresh cherry, to garnish

Add all the drink ingredients to a blender with a large scoop of crushed ice. Blend until smooth. Strain into a tiki glass and garnish with a dehydrated apple slice, desiccated/dried coconut, pineapple spear and a cherry.

HAPPY ENDINGS

Irish Coffee

A cocktail that needs little introduction, the Irish coffee is thought to have been first created by Joe Sheridan at the restaurant at Foynes Airbase, near Limerick, in the early 1940s. The drink was later popularized in the US at Buena Vista Café in San Francisco.

45 ml/1^1/$_2$ fl oz Jameson Caskmates Stout Edition Whiskey

20 ml/^{2}/$_3$ fl oz Demerara/turbinado simple sugar syrup, or to taste

100 ml/3^1/$_3$ fl oz hot coffee

30 ml/1 fl oz double/heavy cream

freshly grated nutmeg, to garnish (optional)

Mix together the whisky, sugar syrup and coffee in an Irish Coffee glass. Place the double/heavy cream in a bowl and whisk until slightly thickened. Using a warm spoon, pour the cream over the top of the drink, creating a foamy 'head'. Garnish with freshly grated nutmeg, if you like.

Cereal Milk Punch

Created by Jeff Bell in 2012 at the famous PDT bar in New York City, this combination of cereal and whiskey works remarkably well.

37.5 ml/1¼ fl oz Bernheim Original Wheat Whiskey

22.5 ml/¾ fl oz Georgia Moon Corn Whiskey

60 ml/2 fl oz Cereal Milk*

15 ml/½ fl oz Bärenjäger Honey Liqueur

freshly grated nutmeg and cornflakes, to garnish

Add all the drink ingredients to a cocktail shaker and shake hard. Single strain into a highball glass over cubed ice. Garnish with nutmeg and a few cornflakes.

*To make Cereal Milk: 120 g/5 cups cornflakes, 1 litre/quart cold whole milk, 35 g/2¾ tablespoons light brown sugar, small pinch sea salt

Preheat the oven to 150°C (300°F) Gas 2. Spread the cornflakes on a parchment-lined baking sheet and bake for 15 minutes. Pour the milk into a jug/pitcher and stir in the baked cornflakes. Let macerate for 20 minutes at room temperature, then strain through muslin/cheesecloth. Whisk the brown sugar and salt into the milk until dissolved. Store in a bottle in the fridge for up to 3 days or until the milk's expiry date.

Spiced Milk Punch

A good drink to enjoy as a nightcap before bed.

50 ml/1⅔ fl oz The Glenlivet 12 Year Old Single Malt Scotch

200 ml/6¾ fl oz whole milk

1 teaspoon light brown sugar, or to taste

1 teaspoon runny honey

1 cinnamon stick

2 cloves

¼ teaspoon ground turmeric

¼ teaspoon freshly grated nutmeg, plus extra to garnish (optional)

Combine all the drink ingredients in a saucepan and heat until just boiling. Remove from the heat and cover with a lid for a few minutes. Strain out the spices and pour into a mug. Garnish with extra nutmeg, if liked.

Hot Toddy

This twist on a classic toddy recipe includes madeira, which works well combined with the whisky's honey, malt and spice notes.

50 ml/1^2/$_3$ fl oz Glenmorangie
The Original Single Malt Whisky
50 ml/1^2/$_3$ fl oz madeira
100 ml/3^1/$_3$ fl oz water
2 lemon slices and 2 orange slices

1 tablespoon unsalted butter
5 ml/1 teaspoon maple syrup, or to taste
pinch of ground cinnamon
cinnamon stick, to garnish

Gently heat all the drink ingredients in a saucepan until warm, then transfer to a toddy glass. Garnish with a cinnamon stick.

Blushing Geisha

This drink is a frozen, blended sazerac of sorts, and is another great example of whisky's versatility in cocktails.

45 ml/1^1/$_2$ fl oz Nikka Coffey
Malt Whisky
10 ml/2 teaspoons fresh lemon juice
20 ml/^{2}/$_3$ fl oz Jasmine Syrup*

3 dashes Peychaud's bitters
3 dashes absinthe
cherry blossom flower, to garnish

Add all the drink ingredients to a blender with a large scoop of cubed ice. Blend until smooth and pour into a rocks glass. Garnish with a cherry blossom flower.

* To make Jasmine Syrup: 500 ml/2 cups water, 500 g/2^1/$_2$ cups caster/ granulated sugar, 20 g/1 cup fresh jasmine flowers

Bring the water to the boil in a saucepan and add the sugar, stirring, until dissolved. Remove from the heat and stir in the jasmine flowers. Allow to infuse at room temperature for 2–3 hours. Strain out the flowers and discard. Store in a bottle in the fridge for up to 1 month..

Irish Flip

The flip is one of the oldest categories of mixed drinks – here we see an Irish take on the classic. Flips were originally served hot, but I find this drink works equally well cold. Similar to eggnog, it's a good drink to serve during the festive season.

50 ml/1²/₃ fl oz Jameson Irish Whiskey
25 ml/³/₄ fl oz Guinness Stout Reduction Syrup*
1 whole egg
10 ml/2 teaspoons Pedro Ximénez sherry
freshly grated nutmeg, to garnish

Add all the drink ingredients to a cocktail shaker with a scoop of ice and shake hard. Single-strain into a wine glass with no ice. Garnish with grated nutmeg.

*To make Guinness Stout Reduction Syrup: 500 ml/2 cups Guinness, 250 ml/1 cup Demerara/turbinado sugar

Put the Guinness in a saucepan and simmer over a medium heat for 30–40 minutes until the volume is reduced by half. Add the sugar and stir until dissolved. Remove from the heat and allow to cool before bottling and refrigerating. Use within 1 month.

CREDITS

The author and the publishers would like to thank all the suppliers who so generously supplied their whiskies used in the drinks and photography for this book.

Brown-Forman
www.brown-forman.com
Woodford Reserve Bourbon,
Old Forester Bourbon

Campari
www.campari.com
Wild Turkey 80 Bourbon,
Wild Turkey 101 Bourbon

CASK Liquid Marketing
www.caskliquidmarketing.com
Mars Maltage "Cosmo" Whisky

Cellar Trends
www.cellartrends.co.uk
Jefferson's Reserve Bourbon

Diageo
www.diageo.com
Bulleit Rye Whiskey

Hi-Spirits
www.hi-spirits.com
Sazerac Rye Whiskey, W.L. Weller
12 Year Old Bourbon, Buffalo Trace
Bourbon, Eagle Rare Bourbon

LVMH
www.lvmh.com
Glenmorangie Original
Single Malt Scotch Whisky

Mariussia Beverages
www.marussiabeverages.co.uk
Rittenhouse 100 Proof Rye Whiskey,
Bernheim Wheat Whiskey, Georgia
Moon Corn Whiskey, Teeling Irish
Whiskey

Maxxium
www.maxxium.com
Maker's Mark Bourbon,
Makers 46 Bourbon

Speciality Drinks
www.specialitydrinks.com
Michter's Bourbon, Michter's Rye
Whiskey, Nikka Whisky From The
Barrel, Nikka Taketsuru Pure Malt
Whisky, Nikka Coffey Malt Whisky

Pernod-Ricard
www.pernod-ricard.com
The Glenlivet 12 Year Old Single
Malt Scotch, Jameson Caskmates
Stout Edition Whiskey, Chivas
Regal 12 year Old Scotch Whisky,
Jameson's Irish Whiskey

Spirit Cartel
www.spiritcartel.com
Four Roses Yellow Label Bourbon,
Four Roses Small Batch Bourbon

INDEX

Benton's Old Fashioned 10
Black Manhattan 28
Blood and Sand 21
Blushing Geisha 61
Bobby Burns 35
Boulevardier 31
Bourbon Spritz 48
Brooklyn 28

Cereal Milk Punch 58

Derby Julep 40

Georgia Mint Julep 40

Honi Honi 25

Horse's Neck with a Kick 52
Hot Toddy 61

Irish Coffee 57
Irish Flip 62

The **K**ingpin 14

Lion's Tail 25

Marquee 48
Mint Julep 39
Morning Glory Fizz 51

New York Sour 18

Paper Plane 21
Penicillin 22
Prohibition Old Fashioned 14

Remember the Maine 31

Sazerac 13
Spiced Milk Punch 58
Sweet Manhattan 27

Tipperary 36
Triple Crown Julep 43

Vieux Carré 32

Ward Eight 18
Whisky Colada 55
Whisky Green Tea 55
Whisky Highball 47
Whiskey Smash 44
Whiskey Sour 17
White Manhattan 32

ACKNOWLEDGEMENTS

Thanks to Don Lee, Jeff Bell and Sam Ross for allowing me to use their recipes in this book. Thanks are also due to all the brands (above) who provided bottles for our photoshoots. Thank you to Mark Jennings for his help in coming up with the perfect title *From Dram to Manhattan*. Last but not least, a big thanks to Joe Stokoe for turning me on to whiskey all those years ago!